B Y

MW00526163

BY A THREAD

MOLLY TENENBAUM

·POEMS·

VAN WEST & COMPANY

SEATTLE

Library of Congress Catalog Card Number: 00–100005

ISBN: 0–9677021–0–0

9 8 7 6 5 4 3 2 1

COVER ART: Karen Yurkovich, *Group of Seven Bonsai*, 1999.
Courtesy of Linda Hodges Gallery, Seattle, Washington.

Van West & Company, Publishers

5341 BALLARD AVENUE N.W.

SEATTLE, WASHINGTON 98117

www.vanwestco.com

ACKNOWLEDGMENTS

THE AUTHOR thanks the journals where these poems, sometimes in other versions, first appeared:

The Beloit Poetry Journal: "Spring Vase," "Every Single Sprout," "As I Set Out," "Neither Now"

Crab Creek Review: "Song for Cellophane and Comb"

Crosscurrents: "Paradise Practice"

Fine Madness: "Reminiscence Forward," "Elephants, Pavilions," "Fluent," "Living inside Green Layers," "The Virtuoso of Field Identification Recognizes a Bird," "A Short History of the Bird Feeder"

Poetry Northwest: "Reading the Atlas: Hydrology," "Saturdays, May to October," "The Hundred-Year Floods That Come Every Year," "Beach Walk and Bad News," "The Spiders in the Fruit of Their Year," "Apple Ladder," "The Tulip Problem," "To the Handsome Young Man Who Bought the Old and Wonderful Picture Dictionary...," "My Lost Apostrophes," "When It Rains, It Pours"

Prairie Schooner: "The Most High Thing"

Seattle Review: "The World Is the Shape of a Cat"

Slant: "Hang Your Clothes on a Hickory Limb"

"Reminiscence Forward" also appeared in *Best American Poetry 1991*.

THANKS ALSO to Kerry Blech and Bob Carlin for helping me trace Marcus Martin, though I may still have it wrong; to Jean, Dan, and Peter for everything; to Mary Jane Knecht for her wholehearted savvy; and to Jenny Van West for loving books.

TO

m.a.t.

1924–1984

CONTENTS

BY A THREAD

THE NIGHT-BASKET

Strawlight in speckle and hexagon
stars your swaying sky

Someone is bearing water perhaps, and you rock
as water lifts in a carried cup

You're daubed in a papery hive,
globed in lantern light

You're latched in dovetailed staves
brushed with steepling hands

You're a windfall, a gleaning, a coal
fanned from the back of a cart

You're a spark when it cools black
and lands, a dot of dark

I

REMINISCENCE FORWARD

We were starving. We had nothing.
But we had bread.
There was nothing to eat.
But there were plenty of tomatoes.
We put the tomatoes on the bread.
We had nothing. But we had garlic.
We would put garlic on the tomatoes and bread.
We were starving, we put olive oil
on garlic, tomatoes, and bread.
There were plenty of tomatoes,
and we ate them on the hillsides,
with garlic and oil and bread.

We were starving. We had nothing.
But we had a cup.
The cup was white inside.
Pink outside.
The pink was a vine of roses.
There was nothing.
There was white. And pink.
And there were leaves.
The leaves were gold paint
in pink roses outside
the white cup. Oh, we had nothing.
The white in the cup, and the pink,
and the gold leaves.

It was empty. There was nothing.
But we had a window.
There were some lines
outside the window, and they were made of wood.
The lines were rails outside the window,
and there were stairs down
that led to fences, and on fencetops
cats walked with their tails,
passing back and forth.
We were starving. There was nothing.
Railings, a window, steps, a view
of fencetops.

Truly we had nothing. Empty, starving, cold.
There was a pond.
We had nothing, truly.
The pond was small.
There might have been something.
But it was small and dark.
We couldn't see, but there were grasses
at the edge: we saw them move,
the water darken.
We had nothing, were so close
to nothing. From our railings,
over our fencetops, while we held
our cup, and ate our oil and bread,
we looked into the pond.
We couldn't see, we had nothing, but it seemed
the blue pond was a thought

that could undo itself
and swim away.

We couldn't see. We were starving.
There was nothing. It was empty.
It was oil and bread.
It was a white cup.
It was railings and fencetops.
It was bluer and bluer.

SONG FOR CELLOPHANE AND COMB

Once in the wide Owens Valley, in lowing wind,
grasses flowing silver, blue, and green,
sky silver, blue, and green, green
tributaries buried in grasses, my shoes
slopped from missing the edges,
I rescued my brother, his head
waving like white heads of grass,

then waving his arms, underwater.
One of us here, another there, each lost
past a bow of the river, in sweeping grass,
our calls thin shavings of wind, me running –

I saw a layer of clear water –
skin there too, floating with clouds,
drifting dimpled green. Perhaps to him
I also gleamed, a shadow with hands,
a tall flute bending. I saw transparency,

nothing so simple or plain
as movement underwater,
or as the thin sheet – clearer, even,
than air – rolling over it, wavy lines
scrolling as the wind smooths by.
Without the sun whiter than any I'd seen,
without the noisy grass, without the twang
of hills to swoop me up ringing, I might not

have run, but did, river swinging
a net of foamed strings on his head
pulling up, river slurring a meadow-swash
up the bank after us. We rode back,
car heat high, motor droning like grass –

and sealed with us, a small gulp of sky
like the blue at the bottom, road zinging white
all around us. Were dried and wrapped warm
so quickly the clangor wrapped with us.
Flat sky and all rhyming land had drummed silver,

bounced us between, but we'd slipped
from the wind's snick and whir
to our own thick wool. I put my head under
to breathe my own breath, but couldn't
believe in saving even then, my brother
snug, the engine under, our speed
like hurtled sleep in the valley's deeper hum.

THE MOST HIGH THING

> "What do you think music is for, Mr. Martin?"
> "Well it's for – it's for – the upbuilding of people. . . . It's
> the highest, most high thing, most high" [*tape cuts off*].
>> – *Fiddler Marcus Martin, interviewed by Alan Lomax for the*
>> *Archive of American Folksong of the Library of Congress.*
>> *Asheville, North Carolina, 1941.*

Once, I heard past pops and scratches
to a single line of clear, pure
music – Salyer's "Lost Boy," folds
and turnings shaking from the bow
like powdered silk, the shivers
smaller than the ear's own coils,
but all at once a loop, a rush,
a cord lifting, to catch, to catch, to catch.

And purchased, once, a sharp, sharp hoe,
cut my fingers opening
the box, cut them again, lifting it out –
a season of thorn and splinter
ends with crosshatched hands, but underneath,
the single fingers, underneath,
the bones, the tune outstretched –

TURTLE STREET

Susie Abraham and I, that afternoon,
lost ourselves dropping in
a shop of cards with gilded roses,
lilac notes embossed
in looping script – *thinking of you* –
while the sign, *Another Time*,
curved over us, a wing
above the door. Weeks after,

from the passing
window of my parents' car,
I scanned the street to catch
that shop again, but never could –
the Pep Boys, yes, hubcap storefront,
everything shiny; and Jack's,
two placards up
that couldn't both be true:
Open Twenty-four Hours,
but *We Never Close* –

And the Apple Pan, yes,
where I begged to stop as we passed by
on errands, me waiting, Mom returning
with blue paper, string, our own
clean clothes like presents.
Though once, years ahead, time slipping
out as we stepped in, Dad
and I sat side by side

at the counter for burgers and pie,
ordinary, good. Not long

after that, he would die. But no
brick-front shop, no arch
inlaid with darker brick,
no fanlight sign – suppose
we'd been inside as it withdrew?
What if, leaving, we'd turned back,
and – blank, a TV blip?

That day with Susie, walking home
past fences, past what glittered
over them like an escalator's
moving edge – sprinkler-water
falling from peaks – across the street,
our same direction, an old man
walked too, his hair
a white so white
it stole his face,

so I ran,
and Susie too, but hard
breath at home, she asked me, Why?

Such danger, Susie, lucky
we could run. This morning
I'd just opened my eyes
and white lilacs
rushed the glass like bombs.

SONG OF CLAY VESSELS

Green cabinet with light-flecked apple handle
Brass terrine with tender dogwood handle
Blue chest, golden pearwood handle
Blue casket, a gentle hazel handle

Red box with stain and black patina
Golden hutch with brown patina
Green teapot with green and rust patina

Reliquary, burnt, with birdlike markings
Copper chest, cuneiform markings
Blue round casket, blue coin markings

Ringlet of a pearwood handle
Curving of a hazel handle
Swinging wand of dogwood handle
Ribboning of apple handle

Brown terrine of baked clay, empty
Cabinet with tall doors open
High chest with knobbed lid set aside

Golden hutch a glowing coal
Casket with a meadow at the bottom
Coffer that unfolds a sheet of wind
Cabinet with high doors open

Curving of an apple handle
Swinging wand of pearwood handle
Ringlet of a hazel handle
Ribboning of dogwood handle

Reliquary with an open palm
High chest with carved lid set aside
Nut-green case with tiny markings
Terrine of breath, the pear, the hazel handles

ELEPHANTS, PAVILIONS

Are they still clouds when they are also towers
of snowball blossom, or cylinders
of wool carding off the mountains?
When I see them as ships and then see only ships
have I trapped my imagination in bays of tiny sails?
When they emerge from shade, blow to shade,
are themselves shade, why do they sing over
and over, *umber, umber*?

Without their windy hair above my hair,
without the rocks of earth their face below my face,
no cradle for my head. Without a sky
weighted like a sagging sheet,
no stopping the atoms of my body from spinning like sirens,
evaporating like playfield cries
from the end of the vanishing street.

If I planted them, what would grow?
Watered them, what would melt?
Sent them letters, what would come back
but puddled glue, and what years would it take
to pat one on the head –
long would the hand ride
like an elevator through stories
of misty hair to rest on something implacable
like a skull, housing for infinite
Magritte of white and blue.

When strings of them horizontally comb,
but one stem frays into a puff,
can we apply theories of fickleness,
or must we give our deepest, in patience and generosity,
to comprehend what wider wind could call a cloud to go?

When they seem thin, what is thinness?
If we stood so, each strand
a grace, our spines adrift,
would our mistakes rain more softly,
our hearts crest and fault enough for love to feather through?

Do they feel it when God burns
ragged at the edges of their holes,
or lays gold jags across their staggered
ranges on an evening's backlit twilight?

Do their fields condense, as earth, to rock?
And in their valleys, where the feet of mountains cross –
if I climb something like a ladder to an upper bunk,
shall I roam the creasing rivers,
round round-shouldered hills, below me spreading
scapes of ploughed hectare and farm?

If I tire, and lay my rucksack on a bank,
pluck a cirrus chewing straw
from this earth beyond my first earth,

if I sleep, counting
like sheep these clouds above my first clouds,

if, when I wake, a glow
sustains the distance,
warmed in the soft-ribbed
valley like a candle in a palm,
shall I know it
for the house where I was born?

READING THE ATLAS: HYDROLOGY

A train-set landscape, cubed
like a block of ice,
cut to cross section and inner works,

sums familiar ground, a gloss
that seems like home:
fences, farms, red barn.

For, as far back as we
remember, mountain snow
has melted to the river,

and this is how we know spring, a trickle
and string of water folding
over itself, pooling

in the reservoir where a thin
sheet spills over
the dam's edge and meanders

through the hills – where nestled flat
and round, like aspirin, the covers of treatment plants
hide rain forests of pipes and tubs and vats

as honest and true as water towers, grain elevators,
telephone poles, railroad ties, and the farmer's well
seen from the side as a long finger

probing the aquifer,
that stoneware bubble of dreams –
shall it be popped?

All this juice and this little
cube of model and the mountain snows wrapped
up in it are hard effort

to not seep dry: in the sky,
as proof, a little plane
sifts silver iodide, for rain.

HANG YOUR CLOTHES ON A HICKORY LIMB

Daughter, fill your coffee can
with salted water. Come,
I'll teach you how to pluck
the snails from garden walls.

The sun is out, the sweet peas breathe
sweet breath, the neighbors' trees
lean in from over, plum
to north, peach to south,

and centered there, the apricots
and moss between the stones.
Plink, plunk perhaps it is
a game; a garden wall

for each: daddy, mommy, little
girl with dog at heel.
Up, and *plunk*. Again, *plunk*.
The deaths so silent

it's hard to believe them –
daddy gone –
plunk – and the dog – and
it's very dark inside the can.

THE VENTRILOQUIST'S GRANDDAUGHTER

A little bird rattles
and trills in a paper sack
he holds open out

the window
over huge
hibiscus flowers

melody quavers
my hair
fluffs the hedge

thinning out
past the park
a tongue pilot-light blue

doesn't talk nor the sharp
orange beak I press
pricking my fingers

on Paradise flowers
each time I come over
we must never sigh

in the milk-drinking game
after sipping keep
quiet but cannot

press here
on my chest
when I breathe

it should move
down for in up for out he says
bird little bird

song like water
caught back of the throat
all the way to Aunt Sadie's

her thumbnail-sweet grapes
Cousin Mayer who naps
glasses on "so I'll see

my dreams" but I never could
find it the muscle
for storing my breath

hand-carved the first Alexander
before I was born was packed up
with a typewriter

shipped from Camp Zachary Taylor
and neither
was ever recovered

Aunt Sadie's last towel
fraying through
a burnt hole in my old quilted pot holder

the next Alexander
John-Henry then Joe
a brain tumor slumped Cousin Mayer

bird little bird
grapes tight-skinned and round
not quite green not quite blue

it was Grandfather's finger
that rattled the bag
but me he had open

the window I'd float
on hibiscus through palms my head
in the swooped path

of birds to the Paradise flowers
behind me he smoothed
out the sack

if I practiced I'd learn
how to breathe then we'd start
but my chest would fly up

he said down so the grapes
I popped for a plump
sour explosion

my bald dead cousin
the watery birdsong
becalmed

in the hollow
breath is not
deep enough to go

FLUENT

The wanting was in me, then moved on.
Behind me closed my first desire, but never
let me go. Even those loves
without forms – softened
as firelit face, edgeless as dawn, blended
as eyelash with shadow – started to shiver, restless,
so I sighed and gave them back, sweeping even
shadow to the walls.
Now when I ask I don't think ahead, but invent
as I go: I'd like coffee, a scone,
I really want a kiss, not just
a kiss, but kisses
that live in sky, whose cirrus roots
don't end, where I would live
wrapped in sky-blue threads.
Each love that enters erases the want
that brought it, then rubs down
a little harder. Whatever rises
disperses, but I put my hand
into the wanting – ground-out trough
for grass-lipped drinkers –
swish, and come up dripping.
And the longing that has looked out of the window
every morning since I was a girl
takes a bend the blue of gravel road:
now the shadow-rolls from the early brush of the broom,
the too-bright tile that's left,
and every kiss that ever landed to me
never happened; any hint of craving

canceled them. And when I raise my fluid hand to wave,
I clear their lingering stain, make more
room for starting over, this time
from before the want began.

॥ II

SATURDAYS, MAY TO OCTOBER

Lettuce – Canasta, Cocarde, Merveille des Quatre Saisons,
    and more
unknowns, but brilliant, brass-red, butter, leaf, Batavian.
And cherries, so plum-fat yellow I'm overcome
with pie-thoughts, pass up raspberries, couldn't cram
cobbler for breakfast, compote for lunch, two kinds
of pie for dinner, and leave room
for bok choy, pea vine, rapini, rocket, mizuna.

Green leaves fountain in my open bags, and I'm deciding
how to talk – burble exuberant colors, or restrain,
one thing so right
the others dry away. Later, blue larkspur sways
inside the fence, but melon-pink poppies buzz
from over, so I can't cross out. I wish
my father alive to help, he'd love
the spinach bouquets so neatly tied, he'd josh
across counters, ask gardener's questions –

by tables of tomato starts, it's him in me
savoring labels: Red Calabash, Brandywine, Brimmer,
him touching Stupice leaves, darker than Romas,
"Called 'potato-leaf,' " the man explains –
no explanation,
but it's good to know. He'd love the paths
the customers draw, leaning forward
for cantaloupe, lifting with both hands,
stem-end to nose, and lowering; love

the resulting tangle invisible as fine fishline
hung up and bangling trees or floating toward
its subtle underwater job. He'd love the booths,
the daughter pricing artichokes. In some twist of time,
I'd be her, summer Saturdays in town to sell

not just these sea-green thistles burnished blue
but Rose Fir fingerling potatoes
to myself, a woman blurred
behind the swinging sacks.
I'd weigh them, and I'd give the change. For my dad,
if no English professor, a farmer, this
workshirted, sunburned man telling his girl
to call it a half-pound even,
though I know it's more.

He'd laugh, baby beets,
clumps butt-side up. He hoped
I'd go to France, the avenues
like paintings, where just standing
on corners you feel the brush
take your hand. But never knew
how near I'd live to market, or that I'd return,
cherry-laden, latent pies, green founts springing, home
through larkspur and poppy,
through the swooning gates.

THE HUNDRED-YEAR FLOODS THAT
COME EVERY YEAR

We expected forsythia first, then plum, lilac, and rose.
We got a blur, as if color had blended to rain.
The days were waves, and we were cells
patterning with other cells – not that we could see
a particular spiral or strange attractor,
but occasionally a tail would flick around a corner,
we might hear a tongue, and those faint senses
may have licked lightly at what we'd been or become,
caboose and window-stained passengers in a tapering
view on the other arm of a curve.
It seemed, when the alarm rang, it was our alarm,
and we were up. It was our job
to pet the cat whether he appeared
as a rock, a small pool, or a vague section
of shade under a tree. Lines were as likely
as other swirls, and we found them in sash and sill,
wavering sieves of the scene. Outside, the rain
poured through our fingers, or our fingers
combed the rain. Our eyes were sky-colored, and the sky –
watered, white, darkening – seemed familiar,
though we couldn't see exactly:
when we rubbed the fabric with finger and thumb,
it fanned into dew. We stood next to the car, ready for work.
Likely, we would arrive there. Possibly, the steering
wheel would blister leaf-bud,
tires root oak, tread crust
rivers of bark. It was our job
to enter the car and drive,

our blood and eyes
as bright as eyes, skin wet
with glistening new green folds –
our job to walk, if that day our legs were water,
if that day our feet were mist, our amble
a billow of particles, wild and white.

THE ORIGINS REMAIN OBSCURE

Though they worried, glancing backward. Folding
the bundles, tightening the straps. Whether
they waited, under a tree, lingered – or not
long enough. If some would stay behind. Though some
had cried all night, and would
continue to cry, casting their clothing,
like tears, behind them. Before anyone
spoke of the particular rose-green, the bitter orange-blue
that brushed them as they arranged themselves,
small ones protected, whether it looked like a plan,
headscarves tied, untied, shifting
feet, impatient, bored. After the last hoisting,
though it was hard to tell, so many
tethers and handles shrugged to fit the shoulder-bumps,
        except
that those rests too would soon rub sore.

When we heard of them again, though we weren't
sure it was them, when we heard that one had seen
a fragrant valley, when we pictured the descent,
some still in tears, red and blue scraps, some
shouting, some continuing to walk. Despite the furrows
they would cut, since our favorite
time began before they left, when ground was sweet,
when milk-sweet air rose up, though ground is now
sweet, milk-sweet air now rises, this
might have been our favorite, if they'd left just
sooner, later. Though the tree remains,
and the air beneath the tree, if their departure

made soft wind, if their imprint
clumped here, knotted there,
rags and sashes like the tail
of some shrinking, unstated kite.

THE UNPAINTED HOUSE

The roof will weep like willow branches,
wooden gutters clog with leaves, water flake
and roll as over a dam, sleek on a consistent
path around one leaf-knot, off
the tip of the one cracking rafter
I bend near at my desk, so these tinny streams
clink behind my left shoulder.

I'll be the one who hears the livelong
slap where drips ply dirt
to gravel, to sand, to a patch of clay;
I might walk through the hall
to the kitchen as light walks through day,
and, rubbing the counters, feel wood
warm to contours of my palm.

I'll be the mailman, shoe bottoms chafing the stairs,
who takes a letter from the clip, and slips another
through the slot. Perhaps the house leans
toward him, slot askew. Perhaps he sees
where by the knob the knuckles
dip the door away, and as he turns he knows
by tough wool at his shoulder
a silvery splinter falls.

I'll be the one – elbows on scoured kitchen table,
ceiling draped over her, cape on a shoulder –
who wipes off the windowsill vases, and then sets them down,
who wipes away seedpods that dry from bouquets,

and wipes along with them, not thinking, some small
grains of wood, the sill
thin as a sugar fingernail, licked.
She's looking out as nothing stops,
and even the most imperceptible change
holds her rapt, so she might live forever.

LIVING INSIDE GREEN LAYERS

Nearest   my trellis of yellowing bean-vines pods
    wrinkling dry and then
the closest tall thing   deodar   needles draping
    the neighbor's beans yellow
too and weighting their sagged netting down
    frondlike foreground
branches veil the neighbor's wisteria-heavy garage but not
    his slatted screen not
his plum tree where escaped wisteria twirls then
    forsythia green fire
above the slats and then so big it crowds my window
    showery three-trunked
birch of the neighbor's neighbor's yard and this
    is all too much
the shapes conjunctions overlaps and then
    the pom-pom top
of a pagoda tree and then a birch on the next block
    shapely   distant   weeping

one red cedar native lacy rounding back

    to vine maple more
accessible than evergreens   sprouting up in human
    lifetimes and like us
perhaps best pulled here beside the beans huge hand-shaped
    leaves begin brown crumpling now

then one fir dark as a story mist rolling
    behind remember

this is in a city among houses then a sweep
   of circle passes
through me in my house to another
   maple volunteer
fat trunk forcing the snaggletooth fence its branches
   by growing damage
the siding but were there no wall I'd reach
   from this desk Michelangelo moment
sap in my arm

   a juniper by juncture
of four fences my vines climb
   its cone and now the three-trunked birch again I can't
see more

   someone looking out at trees might see a rooftop faintly
through a blue spruce
   I can't see I'm under it I hear the neighbor
in his yard his broom
   sweeping his eaves sweep and sweep
under wisteria he sounds
   like trees but I'm by the vine maple penciled
through fringes young
   as if to belong

PARADISE PRACTICE

The day I returned from around the block
where Shayla Blakely had a crippled friend
I told my mom I was crippled and all evening
crawled down the couch up the dinner-chair
afterward brushing my teeth below the sink
spitting out over the bathtub-edge cold
tile hard as my knees but wider the whole floor
to set my pointy bones against

I played braces paper clip across my teeth
it tasted like chard it brought my attention close
pressed sounds out like *fs* wet from my lip
and under my arm an upturned pogo stick
turned crutch for teaching me a limp

I teased the deaf girl at school
whose father bought our class a day
at Disneyland for her birthday
who made us nervous since we worried
for her feelings as we hurt them hoping
her difference kept her from harm

she rounded her mouth but sounds stuck flat
like paper on her tongue her eyes
grew like starfish under her lenses her aids
in plastic flesh tone grayer than flesh proved
she had a casing to crack from while we
of a piece our voices our recess shouts

her real ears pale as leached-out snail shells
I'd find in the garden thin enough
for overcast sun to shine through
parents out the window saw me safe
the pogo right again but couldn't hear
the song I jumped to CRI-pple-I'M-a-CRI-pple-I'M-a
humming until dinner

I'd heard babies who died young enough
could detour straight to heaven
but crawling limping spinning in Wonderland cups
brushing teeth and spitting through invented
braces that hurt wearing them tenderly
everyone else must wait

SPRING VASE

Bleeding heart forget-me-not the world

vase-water a pond the kind concocted
in a jar for home or science class but this one

irreproducibly tangled so lush with cut stem
no one could have made it all I did was fill a cup

all I did want flowers by me where a spider
now continues one leg another intent

who knows if to him the world seems the same green
or stuffier consider Dutch bouquet painters

introducing insects for verisimilitude
surfaces whose lightest white of brushstroke equals crystal

outside in his spider-life he traveled up and down
now in by accident spider-life and all

what enters what leaves won't stay even

the screen door open shut clattering and now
in the waterdrops tense on the petals now in the drops that shake

from the petals more lives
than I see bleeding heart forget-me-not

came in the door what went out
to find them I think of names

for the world shall it be
Spring Vase shall it be O Unimaginably Slender Line

O Sea-Green but Leafing
O Unicellular Flutter Bacteria O

Slipper-Shaped Paramecium (each spider-leg
a host of drops his invisible eyes

like drops while hearts
like baby pocket-watches

pend from green) the screen door swings
I want to forget myself and plants bring me

nearer endless though inches
deep this water in ceramic handwork

glazed and fired I can't forget
myself in what my own hands filled

can't drop in what my own steps lifted through
the door a spring wind bangs today listen

the call from wind to stem
forget and not forget bleed and not to bleed

swing in a row that is not a row
arching line neither arch nor line

O Splash of Pond and Muddy Drop O Continual
Imbalance O All

my banging in and out bearing worlds
I can't see swinging

to empty just color and line then back
to trace twining cause and effect

so locate
me there between root and bloom

somewhere on a stem
my foot just coming in going out the door

forget forget forget forget
cancels or enhances

whatever I am a clear blue
ages pink the petals forget

whatever I am a stem dips
arching pink and white whatever I am

      that banging

EVERY SINGLE SPROUT

Some hunt them at night with flashlight,
    then smash with shovel-back
on flat slug-smashing rock;
    or walk in a still-wet morning
lifting leaves, to slip them like abacus beads
    into fingers themselves like opening flowers;
or bury, lips even with soil,
    jars of beer: hungry,
with their one glue-foot, they'll bumble in.
    Though I hear diatomaceous earth
cuts their coating so they leak from themselves,
    I know eggshells don't work. I know
a lady who swears
    by a mulch of chopped horsehair,
and Ann Lovejoy, who is sometimes
    too cheerful, pays the kids
a penny a slug; yet I know a man
    who attended a lecture where someone said
that freezing pains them least.
    In his freezer we find, despite
his wife's objections, several
    marked plastic tubs, inevitable
winter carried
    into deeper sleep.

I choose morning before dew dries,
    pick them like fruit, like overripe
berries that must
    be drawn by the barest of pressures

off the briar that wants
    to keep them. I can't help it, I admire
their shapes, one like a plum seed,
    but fatter, lines on the sides
like the stripes leading back
    from the corner of a kitten's eye;
one with the spotted grace of a leopard,
    slender as a salamander, lucent glossy brown.
The ugliest's a raw lump, like a fingertip
    cut off, beginning to unform,
or fresh uncolored matter left over,
    flung into lavender evening
with God's last shake before
    he ducked inside for dinner.

Yet the book, in diagram's black line, gives them all
    equally well-defined innards: a nerve-ring, a crop, a
        stemlike
esophagus; and zooms in with electron-scan
    of radula – think of a belt-sander,
but with teeth; and though naming names,
    L. maximus, A. rufus, D. reticulatum, resorts at last
to "gray field slug,"

    so doesn't help me as I practice
seeing something small and young and new, something
    barely figured on mica-flecked ground,
like dirt itself, and glistening, that even so,
    grinds black-eyed Susan before
she sprouts leaves to live, lets by
    a few, eats those – she fails from exhaustion,

can't keep up. I learn to see pale crescents
    like the nail parings of infants, prick them up
with the tip of my own bigger nail;
    and like dew, like seed pearls, others stick
to my hand as it brushes a leaf –
    as if they
wanted me.

    Without them, would I rise
each morning, yard in danger
    if I don't? Strawberry-red, the new rose
hangs a blurry sun above the grass.
    Stems and undersides, contrasts
matte and glossy green, the soft blooms lean. By June,
    they're bigger than berries, and dry ground
prevents them from traveling far,
    though still I rise as if theirs is a sweet gift
of silver-trail, of every rescued color –
    magenta glow, unraveling gray,
the swirling, wet light
    newly opening, scalloped away.

AS I SET OUT

Today I toss a wish in my Perhaps Bag
    before setting out,
and I put cheese and bread together,
    seal them in my plastic sandwich box,
and tumble these
    together with the wish
inside the dark Perhaps Bag.

Today I pat my shoes to fit my feet,
    place shoe and foot together on the step,
bread and cheese and wish banging my hip
    through the bag's soft cloth as I set out.

Today I slip my eye in place under my glasses,
    then stand back, allowing eye through glass
to light on blooming doublefile viburnum,
    a tree whose name I have just learned;
so name and eye and glasses bob above
    the foot and shoe, while in between
the wish and sandwich bounce,
    Perhaps Bag at my hip as I set out.

Today as I set out, I add the bird
    leaving the birch,
whose crossing to the roof seems such hard work,

suspension using every ounce of wing.
I add the white bar and black head
    of another bird, small, but weighing
just enough to twitch bright arcs from highest hemlock
    branches.

Today I'd planned to pack the fewest needed things.
    I'd eat the sandwich, I'd remove the shoes,
but keep the eye, for looking later where the day had gone,
    how it had started with a wish,
how wish and sandwich rubbed –

But I added birds and trees with names,
    and I collected on my way small garden jobs to tuck
        somewhere,
and hoped to manage this as simply
    as I'd tucked the eye snug in its eye spot,
fit the foot, extending in its shoe:
    trim the sorrel, weed the stones,
clear tall clutter from clean lines of iris bed –
    though in bare dirt, a new small clutter grows.

Today when I came home, I opened the bag that had flapped
    beside me all day, shook crumbs
from the sandwich box, washed it, leaned it up to dry.
    And as I walked by the open bag, not looking
down, I saw with sight like muffled hearing,
    sight like the sound of a roundness pressing the air –

saw the farthest corner darkest,
    saw the shape of something without corners,

    where I'd tossed it when I started.
    Beside me all day,
    between eye and shoe,
    small as a burn
    in a purse, and swinging
    in soft cloth as I set out.

NEITHER NOW

All summer I lived in the bees' house,
but by then it wasn't I,
it was what the bees flowed by,
what they danced
some distance from. What they didn't notice,
coming and going.

As if the house were a crystal trellis,
palmfuls of tigereye, amber
invested the walls.
Behind Father's portrait grew singing,
his young face a surface of singing.
Humming made a halo of the frame.

Outside the hole, air like smoke,
the siding stained like smoke.
What did I do for bones,
giving the house away?
I lived in a bowl of bees,
I lived where light
caught in hairs, like beads.

One day I followed two blue lines –
behind me the velvet poppy closed.
How occupied I bent there, filling my pockets.

Saw shapes come and go,
one in a dark jacket.

Seedheads swell, the slightest wind
taps seed like spilling loam —

is that my hair, grown long now?
A dried petal
in my multiform eye?

❧ III

THE VIRTUOSO OF FIELD IDENTIFICATION
RECOGNIZES A BIRD

From the footprint like a face in grass the watcher left,
    taking his binoculars, and from the leather flux of the strap
    at dawn before the bird.

From hair like footprinted grass the leather-soft wind
    parted on a man before he could see
    in the light, on the day of the bird.

From the flutter like wings the top of a head casts to sky,
    and from the vehemence or carelessness,
    melancholy or nonchalance
    with which the man re-combs his hair
    after the breezy bird passes.

From the open keyhole of weather, its blue wing
    spooning the rags of clouds.

From threads of an aria over and over,
    curtaining from a window like blue between clouds
    on a billowy evening of birds.

From the degree the trail of dark resembles the wandering aria,
    but darker, deeper,
    and from the angle of spoon
    in the slow bowl of bedtime
    at night in the town of the bird.

From the degree to which night is an impenetrable solid or
     a spacious
    infinity like an emptied bowl
    upturned over an arm outstretched
    in sleep, in the black of the bird.

From the bright afterimage gold in the eye,
    and chance gold recurring
    later when a walking woman's casually tossed
    hair takes the shape of a wing or wedge
    but falls straight again, with no one seeing.

From the walking that won't shake it off,
    the triangular wedge, the taking and leaving of shapes,
    the shadowy pressure near or ahead,
    wherever the next step will be.

BEACH WALK AND BAD NEWS

We are not at either end
of time, beside the big blue eye,
the widest light that opens
back to blue. Pebbles have not yet ground
to sand, nor are they melded
still in one smooth slope of stone. *Now* is
small things like the glass,
brown necks of bottles, green fragile
sides of bottles, sticks cracked off logs, splinters
teased from sticks, and single suns
cupped on water in a hollow shell.

And what of all this is debris,
will not feed some insect, air, some anagram
with wings, or some sweet wrack
farther than sight;
what is not scenery,
piled right up to the top
cliff boundary where shrubs continue
creaking as the wave slaps in?

Let's not call the barnacles
on that last rock tenacious, their closed beaks
a squinting face or amazing
sexual part, wonder of mechanics.
We might try not to imagine
what cracks of sky their doors
let in, or how it feels, like a cool basement
on a hot day, when waters eddy

soft into their chambers;
or not to guess, if a chunk of shore should thrust
and orphan them on mountains,
how long they'd wait, or if they'd ever know
the sea will not come back.

    We might say they stand on their heads
and kick their food into their mouths,
if we can match their flesh and bone
to head or foot or mouth. Walking
at the rim of that big lapping
eye, on shining glass, among the gleams
of whitened wood, we might try not
to call them anything. But pressing
their craters and rubbing the rocks
where they've left rough and starry rings,
we won't help it.
Not tenacious, not clever
to feather supper from the tide,
not foolish or wise to cling or stand –
but at least they're hungry,
curled in salty houses. At least, hard.

THE SPIDERS IN THE FRUIT OF
THEIR YEAR

A strand loops like a watch-chain in the open workroom
      window,
but when the cat leaps up, lands, leans out to smell the new
      fall air,
it breaks across his orange breast, springs up, invisible.

Another snaps when I swing the back door through it,
unaware, on my way out.

Dust-hung webs, like hammered shields, shimmer by tomato
      row –
I squeeze sideways, under, emerge
like something from a web, dragging thread,
tomatoes glowing in my hands.

My blind feel
with scissors along a dahlia stem
to find the base and cut the flower
crashes canopied and understoried layers,
my hand sticky hours after.

Webs tickle my shoulder as I tend the rose,
mustache me bending to the asters,
and one I crush against the faucet
when I turn the hose to water one last time this year –

and in the wood-grain of the garden gate, the miracles
  of chance
have left one cat hair stuck straight up,
and off its tip, one half-seen swoop ascends,
while in an ignored garage-door corner, short lines press,
like half-transparent felt, and inner wrappings
coat what look like brownish peas
but may be husks of eaten things,
or else the new, now swelling to be born.

The spider in the open workroom window casts again,

incandent legs like catch-hooks on a seed.
But the tomato-spiders wait,
brown and furry, fat like fruit.

A frond of down – carelessly shed? flown up from flurries
  with the cat? –
catches in the open workroom window, blows,
and now a net of invisible silver stretches across the breast of
  the cat,
now receives me, fallen through the back door to the world –

to be wrapped white and set to sway,
to dangle, dry and bleached and light.
All the floating fronds wind thick, the house a spool,
the door we never use now woven shut.
I'd like to see the whole house like this,
elaborately trilled in threads and dirt,
shining with dust.

APPLE LADDER

Slimmer than
a lancet arch,
ascending scant,
tapering, then
just air; and lovely
leaning in trees,
lovely leaning
bare by the house,
rungs and clapboards
aligned, side rails
tense with upwardness,
the stronger across
the more the green
wood dries.

And so our grasp
of all, our reach
to gather, climb
to view, our stand
above the orchardslope
could be as lovely,
twined in leaves,
contained as ladders
in themselves,
and light
as ladderwood.

As if, though slung
with heavy sack,

we pause, don't ache
to put it down,
or press for more,
but stand half-high,
our footings half-
obscured by grass,
at our cheeks
half-shaded curves
of fruit, above
our heads, ripe sun,
and crowns of more fruit hanging.

A SHORT HISTORY OF THE BIRD FEEDER

The first were stubbled fields,
fall corn shocks, busted sacks along the old mill road.
A granddad with bread chunks took the kids from underfoot,
and later a man from the new entrepreneurial classes
walked out from his still-sticky manse, bent under
a miniature castle, seeds dripping from its windows
down his elbows, suet battlements
melting like sweat down his brow.
Wandering the story too is Hansel:
if not for the woodsman (who chops
nests along with trees), he'd be gingerbread
on vanishing paths, pecked bits, sogged gunk,
dissolved, disguised as leaves.

Mine's a plexitube with steel-rimmed holes,
made by "Droll Yankee," which I hope I'm not,
purveyed by Audubon, that society born
of mixed feelings, love's and painting's
crossed needs. Now that I've started,
I can't stop, or hundreds
of birds may die. They took two days
to find it, but now the tube's bare-whistle clean
by midmorning. I shouldn't be messing
here at all, but even in Olduvai
birds picked bones, and now
I've got these rushed mornings, twisting worry
I'll forget, change, pass
the yard to strangers.

I don't love birds.
Buff breasts, black caps, like shining
seeds themselves, they pour down perches,
then flow up again, like illusion.
Showing pale underwings, rising,
returning, the whole cavortle
a shimmy in midair – I love
the twitter, sudden flits
all rising in soft language. Whoever sliced
fluttering pages, clutched them out
through unmonitored exits, yes
it's the flutter that gets me, when they land.
What I've got myself into,
breaking as they go.

THE TULIP PROBLEM

Tell me, they've opened?

    Buds to cups to palms

And in?

    Calico directions, wide
    to window, full
    to room, some straight up,
    all with questioning

Looks, like the cat, with cocked ears?

    Yes, and creased leaves like tongue's
    in-between genetics,
    some curl, and others –

Great, but you're forgetting important –

    Colors, I can't
    speak fast enough, clear red, like straight
    food color, now clotted
    dark, older, and stamens
    black like animal eyes
    and rounded hips white but I don't

Remember how that happened?

Flower soaked pure red
at first. Perhaps –

Relax. Try leaping ahead –

I will. Blue yard-sale find
stamped "Perfect" in glass cursive,
mason jar crowds
stems at squeeze point

Magnifies below?

like pressure to tell you this,
to notice how above the rim
a yellow wither has begun
without my catching the moment
it seeped in, caught on.

Say it, lazy, you wish –

Yes, I'm sorry, I wish
they'd last.

And look what you've left out. No mention

Of purple? What could I do,
mouth so full of red?
But one sticks farther out of the jar than the others and
each petal has a dark seam, like lips, in the middle, and
some are crinkled as if starting to cry, but
one bud anomaly has begun

the drain to transparency without ever opening –
you're getting impatient

Are you getting somewhere?

This whole vase and caboodle
on the sill next to dried bay leaves
from a friend who gathered

Anything fits, I know, but

them in California mountains,
now posied in a jar named "Very organic
peaches in honey," that someone else
brought dahlias in

So many jars –

And next to a home-blessing candle
from the same friend who gave me a hummingbird votive
(Miracle Candle Company, Laredo, Texas)
when my heart was broken

You're getting out

Of hand, yes, but what
about window blinds banding translucent
petals, or the house across the street
with similar blinds, or that tulips near
loom larger than that house

Calm, calm – you can come to a close wherever you are.

    I wish they'd never, but I love
    what's left when petals go:
    sticky, ridged, exposed

Table scattered with scraps?

    Husks and winter debris

So, finished?

    A cluttered sill, but through the vase, a scene
    of stems, and January sun flows down the eave
    of the garage, melts all over
    grass at the curb, I'd keep talking,
    but as if a funnel-tip attracts
    the runny light from somewhere down the block

The only way to make you stop. Everything goes

    Narrow, where I can't see it anymore.

Washed clean?

    Threads of water from the sponge
    on the pollen-drifted table
    have dried smooth, but sunset tapers
    shadows of seeds and dried curls
    to inverse flashlight beams,
    filament but invisible

kitchen web from stove ring and doorjamb
to spider down the basement stairs, a very fine tangle
like mist or bright sun,
blind at the doors of the rooms.

TO THE HANDSOME YOUNG MAN WHO BOUGHT THE OLD AND WONDERFUL PICTURE DICTIONARY AT THE BOOK SALE BEFORE I EVEN SAW IT, AND GAVE ME A GLIMPSE OF IT AFTER

In the beautiful rows, across and down,
marvels and lines can crack right through
overwild imagination: there's an Arm
with elbow dimple, there's a two-ended Bone.
Throw me the milk-biscuit and have done;
give me these Crutches, delicately engraved,

and these knobbed and crafted staves,
and on every page, emblems so evenly placed
they can be counted backward, like a careful coin collection:
Zinnia, Yacht, and Xenium, imbricates
of petal, towers of sail, shining bowls
for gift and grape. But you, walking away,
show me what they drew for Deity,
and did they Etch Empiricism with liquid falling
from the lips of crystal beakers?

Draw what I can say, and I'll Follow
you and your chaw-colored book
over Woodpiles, through Wringing and Weirs;
I'll Visualize, fingermark by fingermark,
lip-reading this alphabet embossed
in penny signs, their heads and tails.
At once I'll Unbutton and Unify
if you Teach me to Generalize this Tangle

of ink for Hope, and lead me by the finger-scan
through your apartment door to the Inside
of everything Inevitable.

And once we're settled on the couch,
I'll ask: Did they manage every shine of Twinkle?
Did they show Star to say the gazer?
Are arrows allowed?
For Stink was it a nose?
For Rebate, a car, or wallet
of enlivened, widened powers?

For Jazz, was it a saxophone, could music come ungloved?
For Jehovah, was the space a blank of awe?
For Kilowatt-hour, lightbulb plus a clock,
a Rebus of electrocuting tick and slump?
For Landmass, what great weights
did they delineate, and was Quite
a mouth, primmed up with bright
Quintessence?

And who, young man, are you,
Purist of the book-sale law
that grabbing leads to Owning, and if you Own,
you're Nibbled, Noble
all over? You have parted the Middle
of the book and Marrowed me
in Marsh Marigolds, their haze

hung everywhere: each figured bit
of light a coin, coins for pages by the pound,

every pound a pupil's gleam,
and every gleam the cherry stain
a sweet leaves on the tongue.

MY LOST APOSTROPHES

Oh, you specks, fine spice.
You're the flags of thirty-second notes
flipping fast, you're mockery's
graffiti mustache, you're bad taste's insistent
belly-poke, you're eyebrows raised,
you're the cough after a bad joke.

You're a carob pod, rattled. A mule's
jawbone, hoedown time.
Your fiddlesticks don't let up, you're my last
y's descender, the trim
on my crossed *t*. When time has gritted
stone, you're 'tone, you're a bell's
clapper, you're its staving rim,
you're its ring, hill-kissed, and the cling
of the ringing's final wave.

Once I pressed you like a tack
to plaster, now tacks fall, I'm duff,
I'm frangible wall. With you, there go
friend and *necessary*, all my old mnemonic tricks.
Friend ends, *necessary*'s a princess.
Pepper, you're cracked.

There goes the page's navigation,
what to count, the dark or white.
I ride spaces down
that ravel like rivers, strands
that plait the page with light.

Its' a word now. It's my fault
for obscure examples: not
cat's fleas, but *fleas' hunger*.
Tweaked dot, you're the cat's itch.

You're *hamantasch* filling. You're Grandmother's
burnt wick. You're the candle
at both ends, you're a cranky
old beach stick. "Dark and bizarre,"
says the field guide, you're on the head
of a Harlequin duck. You're tossing turbs
in a wild mountain stream, you're swimming
to winter's slurred habitat,
coast waters, rough.

One stroke,
another. You're castanets.
You're the squirm at the edge of a glaucous eye,
a squiggle of escaping batter, fried.
You're the feeder's black seed,
the crow's nipped worm,
the rain of split hulls.
You're for the birds.

You're French and stylish, in cafés.
You make a page of vowels Hawaiian.
You're for increasing collections – see Getty's Museum.
You're my subtractions: black to 'lack,
whole to 'hole – a brief olé,
extremities cracking like candy.
Once I had a raisin eye, a licorice nose.

Pecked out. You scattered cloves,
you Hellespont. I'm 'o'.

BY A THREAD

When the flowers could move
through the fields to visit each other,
long before there were people,
even the old now don't remember,

when the moon was the sun's lover
and curled inside him like bones,
how there was and there wasn't,
when the dark was clay as soft

as dough, when the light, as harsh
as yellow soap, startled the branches
to glow like veins, in the days
of our great-grandfathers,

seven hundred, eight hundred, maybe
nine hundred years ago, in the golden holiness
of a night that will not be seen again –
I was there, blowing the coals

for bread. I saw and heard it all.
But I was hungry, tried to steal
a crumb, had to run
through crooked trees,

losing my pockets as I went,
so cannot bring you proof
of my story. But it was so,
and here you are, and now

you'll sleep, for if this evening
had not been, this tale
would not have been, and if
this tale had not been, this evening

would be lost. Not you with your head
on the pillow nor I with the song
by your head could ever
thread our ways to find it.

THE WORLD IS THE SHAPE OF A CAT

When you tramp the high gales of night,
when you walk the vault of starry sky,
when every bound leaps you over a tall black hill,
you're high in the hump of her black shoulder;
when you smell the pliant folds
of blue plum leaves, when you scent willows
twitching at the faintest breath of light,
you're in the haze of her meadowy ear;
when you traverse the field's expanse,
from stipple and blade through the long sway
to haying, you're a speck that casts
a shadow on her dreaming haunch,
a gold and rippling
continent as broad as wind.

When you shinny pollen through a valley churned,
a broth rich as the sea, your sneeze
ruffles the shag of her back leg;
when you upturn the last
dark row of bottomland against
the mountain's granite, flowering
white beyond, you walk the clasped
enclosure of her tail; and raking
speckled dirt, you're in the mole-soft
skin of her black toes.

When you, looking the other way, just glimpse
a cutout on the sill, a stamp

to see through where she used to be,
you're at the sharpened
pupil of her daylight eye;
and when the pungence
of one hillside's sage is more
than you can bear, you're the kite
of her nostril, coasting the dusty heat down.

When you come upon a heap
of oak leaves blushed with mold
at the cracked foot of a tree
as cold begins; when you come back
to that same place in spring, dirt wet
as newborn worms; when you can't help
but curl there in a summer's
dappled nap – you're where the sun
rides light-tipped sky, and slides
the rivels down,
and finds a bed of dust to warm,
and finds the secret
of her sleep.

WHEN IT RAINS, IT POURS

My father's name was Morton, so the little girl,
her yellow dress on rain-drilled blue,

was me. The same way "You Are Here" signs knew,
the Salt People, from where they were, could tell

what our rain would do. He sang
"Sweet Afton," strewed my bedtime's sifting

story of Tolly and Kay, their friend Crazy Tree with a door
at the root up to hundreds

of rooms: forest room – flickery, dim;
ocean room – foamed sandy-blue; sleeping room –

frilled like another girl's
bedroom might be, gauzed windows as white

as the drizzle hummed over, on, in me. And inside
the highest, most shivery twig, a meadow

for picnics, tall grass all the way
to pure sky, and sprinkles

of yellow-white flowers. I put deviled eggs
in the story to match. And woke, the first one

in the kitchen, where tiny holes
in the shaker made powder, where threads

of the opening top
ground caught salt finer.

Saw seven rice grains,
yellowy, clear.

Just in case, just in case, called my mom –
though with bare feet on linoleum, early,

I'd seen the Salt Girl, deep blue,
in splashes like stars. She'd be wherever I'd look,

beside me on swings, in stove-steam.
A king's third daughter, I'd heard,

loved him as meat loves salt, so youngest
was secretly luckiest. I would be her,

rain-flecked song, swish, like the scent
through our screens, my father's

alyssum, his lavender, rose.
They could have dipped

their salt fingers in anywhere, and found a stream –
through breezeways, through whispery

metal spouts, among the green braes, up to shimmering
pastures through a little door – it always

poured. The softness,
the girl's yellow dress. And I had a clear self

to keep myself in, a me not me –
like the hag who, at night before bed, poured magic

in her golden little finger, unscrewed it, and slept
with it under her head; like the young man

who kept Death in a sack he hid high in a tree
till they begged him – *Open it.*

NOTES ON THE POEMS

THE MOST HIGH THING: Marcus Martin (born in 1881 in Macon County, North Carolina) was recorded for the Archive of American Folksong during several sessions in 1941, 1942, and 1946. In the late 1960s or early '70s, collectors ordered copies from the Library of Congress, and eventually tapes of this elegant fiddling began circulating among old-time musicians. John Salyer, legendary fiddler of eastern Kentucky (born in 1882 on the Birch Branch of the Burning Fork of Licking River), was recorded by his son. A cassette is available: *John Morgan Salyer: Home Recordings 1941–1942* (Berea, Kentucky: Appalachian Center AC003, 1993).

SONG OF CLAY VESSELS: After ceramics by Roz Barnett of Seattle, Washington.

HANG YOUR CLOTHES ON A HICKORY LIMB:

> "Mother, may I go out to swim?"
> "Yes, my darling daughter.
> Hang your clothes on a hickory limb,
> And don't go near the water."
> – #879 in *The Annotated Mother Goose*
> (William S. and Ceil Baring-Gould, New York:
> Meridian Books, 1967)

The Baring-Goulds' annotation points to P. A. Ditchfield, who, "in his book *Old English Customs*, states that this jingle is thirteen hundred years old, and that it was first recorded in a book of sixth-century jests compiled by one Hierocles."

EVERY SINGLE SPROUT: "The book" is *Terrestrial Slugs*, by
N.W. Runham (London: Hutchinson, 1970).

APPLE LADDER: After a ladder built by George Ainley of
Perkinsville, Vermont.

BY A THREAD: "If he hasn't died, he's living today." "I was
there and now am here." "They lived well in those days, and
we live even better." These phrases, as well as many in the
poem, are spoken by the Gypsy storytellers in Diane Tong's
Gypsy Folktales (New York: Harcourt Brace, 1989) as they
open and close their tales. I tried to hide phrases of my own
among theirs.

THE WORLD IS THE SHAPE OF A CAT: Nellie-Ivy, glimmer-
ing tortoiseshell, 1984–1989.

ABOUT THE AUTHOR

MOLLY TENENBAUM lives in Seattle, Washington, where she teaches creative writing and plays traditional string band music. She is the author of *Blue Willow*, recipient of the 1998 Floating Bridge Press Poetry Chapbook Award, and her poems have been published widely in literary magazines and anthologies, including *Best American Poetry* 1991, *Poetry*, *The Beloit Poetry Journal*, *Poetry Northwest*, and *Prairie Schooner*. Her banjo playing appears on several recordings of traditional American old-time music, including *And the Hillsides Are All Covered with Cakes*, *The Young Fogies II*, and *Race the River Jordan*.

BOOK DESIGN and composition by Jennifer Van West, using Adobe PageMaker 6.5 and a Macintosh 7500. The text type is Bembo with Poetica titles and ornaments. *Printed by McNaughton & Gunn.*